Sort by One Attribute

Draw lines from the animals to their homes.

Circle the animal in each row that does not belong.

 To find out some of the ways animals are sorted, or classified, make a trip to a library or bookstore. Look for books on amphibians, dinosaurs, Arabian horses, pets, or any other animals that interest you.

1

Sort by **One Attribute**

Sort by Two Attributes

1. Draw lines from the big bears to one basket. Draw lines from the little bears to the other basket.

2. Sort the bears another way. Draw lines from the bears to the boxes to show how you sorted them.

Draw some bears. How many different ways might the bears be sorted?

2

Name _____

Sort Fractions

1. Find the shapes that have two parts.
   Color one half **red**.
   Write $\frac{1}{2}$.

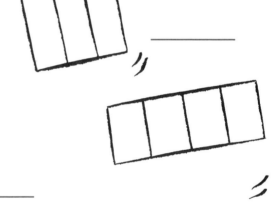

2. Find the shapes that have three parts.
   Color one third **blue**.
   Write $\frac{1}{3}$.

3. Find the shapes that have four parts.
   Color one quarter **green**.
   Write $\frac{1}{4}$.

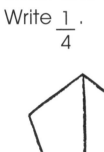

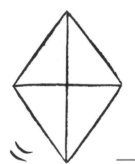

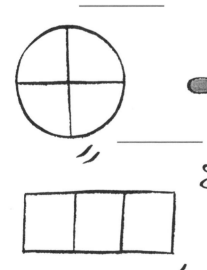

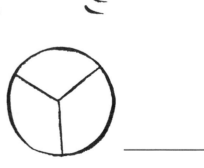

Name the shapes on this page.

3

Classify Figures

Squares, triangles, and other plane figures are flat.

Solid figures are not flat. Everyday objects are shaped like solid figures. For instance, balls are spheres and cans are cylinders.

Plane Figures   **Solid Figures**

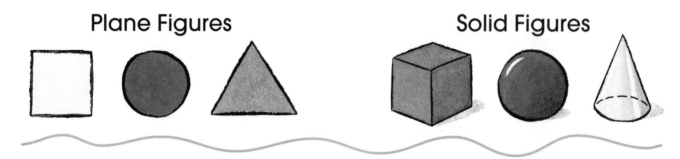

Circle the figure in each row that does not belong.

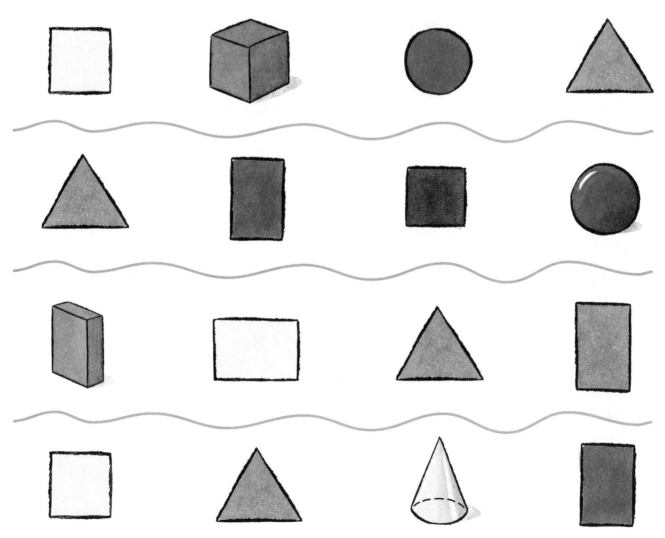

Match Objects to Solids

Draw lines from the objects to the matching figures. An example is done for you.

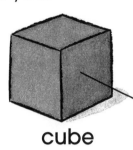

cube

cylinder

sphere

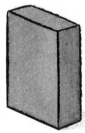

rectangular prism

cone

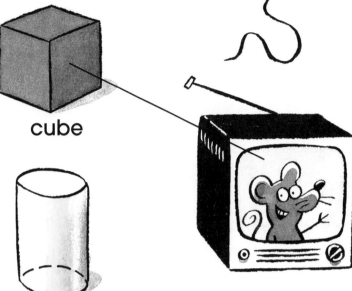

Picture Graphs

This picture graph shows how many birds these children saw one morning.

Number of Birds						
Kyle	🐦	🐦	🐦	🐦	🐦	🐦
Jan	🐦	🐦	🐦			
Paco	🐦	🐦	🐦	🐦	🐦	
Sara	🐦	🐦	🐦	🐦	🐦	🐦 🐦

Each 🐦 stands for 1 bird.

1. How many birds did Paco see? _____

_____

2. Who saw the most birds? _____

_____

3. Paco saw more birds than _____ .

4. How many birds did Paco and Kyle see together? _____

 Look out a window and count the number of birds you see in 15 minutes.

Name _____

Tables and Picture Graphs

The table shows how many bird nests each child saw.

Draw s in the picture graph to show how many nests each child saw.

Number of Nests	
Kyle	6
Jan	3
Paco	1
Sara	3

Number of Nests	
Kyle	
Jan	
Paco	
Sara	

Each stands for 1 nest.

1. Who found the most nests? _____

2. _____ and _____
found the same number of nests.

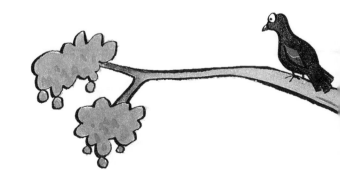

Picture Graphs

This is a picture graph about the weather in April.

sunny	☀	☀	☀	☀	☀	☀	☀	☀	☀	☀	☀	☀
rainy	💧	💧	💧	💧	💧	💧	💧	💧	💧	💧		
cloudy	☁	☁	☁	☁	☁	☁	☁	☁				

0   1   2   3   4   5   6   7   8   9   10   11   12

Number of Days

1. On how many days did people need an ☂ ? _____

   _____

   Why? _____

2. On how many days would you wear 👓 ? _____

   _____

   Why? _____

3. What kind of weather happened least during April?

   _____

   _____

Keep track of the weather for one week. Tally the various types of weather and tell which kind of weather happened most often.

Name _____

Tally Marks and Bar Graphs

This table shows some children's favorite kinds of pets.
Each tally mark shows one child's vote. Count the tally
marks. Write the totals.

	= 1 vote ЖЖ = 5 votes

Pets	Votes	Totals
birds	ЖЖ	
dogs	ЖЖ |||	
fish	|||	
cats	ЖЖ ||	

1. How many like birds best? _____

2. How many like dogs best? _____

3. How many like fish best? _____

4. How many like cats best? _____

Fill in the bar graph with the information from the table.
The birds are done for you.

Votes for Favorite Pets										
birds										
dogs										
fish										
cats										

0   1   2   3   4   5   6   7   8   9   10
Number of Votes

5. Which kind of pet is the children's favorite? _____

Tally Marks

Look at all the toys! Let's count them.

Tally each toy. Then write the number.
The balls are counted for you.

| | = 1 toy | 卌 = 5 toys |

		Tally Marks	Number
	balls	卌 卌	10
	bears		
	cars		
	games		

Make a tally of CDs, books, stuffed animals, or another group of belongings.

Bar Graphs

Use the table to complete the bar graph.

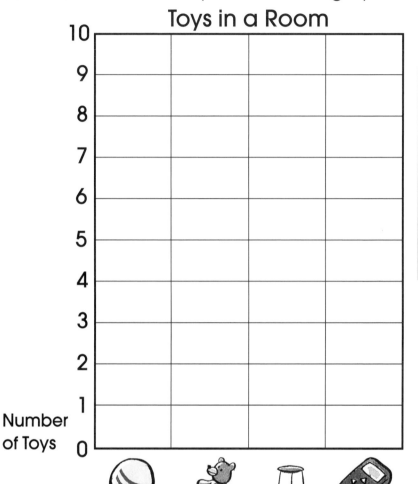

Toys in a Room

Number of Toys

balls   bears   cars   games

Toys	Number
Balls	10
Bears	7
Cars	6
Games	9

_____

_ _ _ _ _ _ _ _ _ _ _ _ _ _ _ _ _

1. Which toys are shown the most? _____

2. How many more s than 🚗s?

_____ − _____ = _____

3. How many 🏐s and 🚗s together?

_____ + _____ = _____

     Bar **Graphs**

Tally Marks

Tally the coins in the bank. Then write how many.

quarter

25¢

dime

10¢

nickel

5¢

penny

1¢

Coins	Tally Marks	Number
pennies		
nickels		
dimes		
quarters		

Bar Graphs

Use the table to complete the bar graph.

Coins in the Bank						
pennies						
nickels						
dimes						
quarters						

0   1   2   3   4   5   6

Coin	Number
pennies	4
nickels	3
dimes	6
quarters	2

1. There are more _____ than pennies.

2. There are more nickels than _____ .

3. How many coins? How much money?
   The pennies are counted for you.

_____4_____ pennies   Count by 1s. $ _0.04_

_____ nickels   Count by 5s. $ ___.___

_____ dimes   Count by 10s. $ ___.___

_____ quarters   Count by 25s. $ ___.___

Total Amount $ ___.___

Coordinate Graphing

Use the grid on the map to find the treasure.

To find the clock, start at 0. Go across to E and up to 1.

Circle the treasure you find at the letters and numbers below.

1. C, 4

2. E, 1

3. B, 0

4. C, 2

Write the letters and numbers to find each treasure.

5. _____ _____

6. _____ _____

7. _____ _____

8. _____ _____

Study highway maps. Use map grids to find your town or city and places where people you know live.

Coordinate Graphing

This map shows where you can find things in a park.

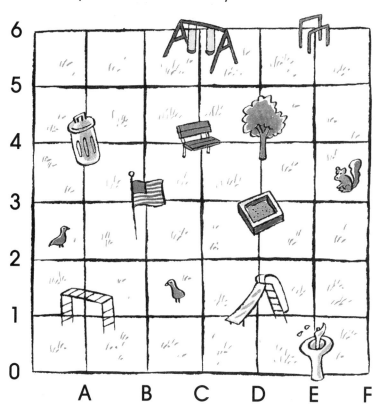

Where is the bench?
Go across to C.
Go up to 4.

Find each thing in the park. Write the letter and number.

1. _____ _____

2. _____ _____

3. _____ _____

4. _____ _____

5. _____ _____

6. Follow these directions:
   Start at 0.
   Go across to A.
   Go up to 2.
   Go across to B.
   Go up 1.

   What do you see?

   _____

   - - - - - - - - - - - - - - - -

   _____

 Draw a map of your yard or part of a park. Then have someone use the map to find a certain feature or object.

15   Coordinate **Graphing**

Classify Objects as Solids

Circle the objects that have the same form as the figure in the first box.

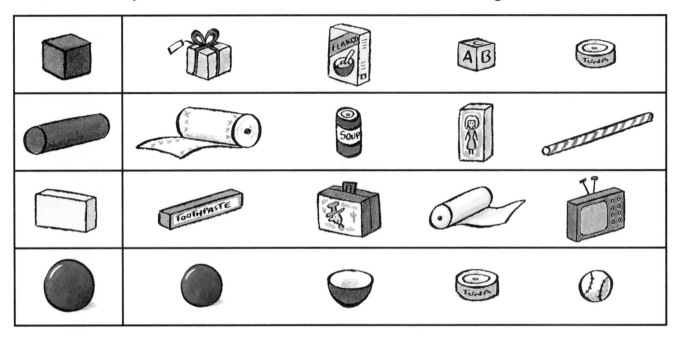

Read the names of the figures. Then cross out the objects whose forms do not match.

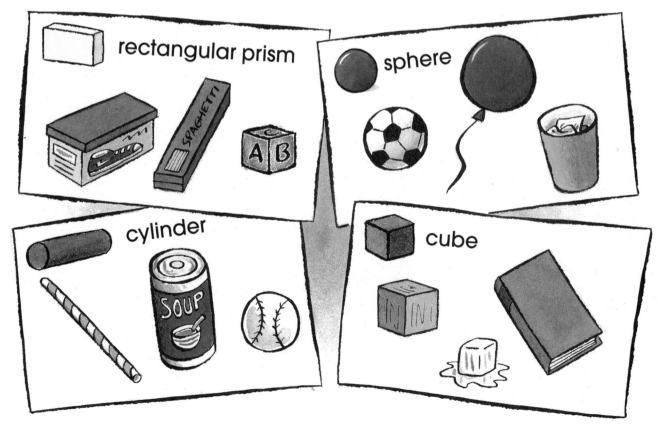

Sort Solid Figures

 stack  slide  roll

Circle each figure that will stack.

Circle each figure that will slide.

Circle each figure that will roll.

Circle each figure that will slide and stack.

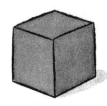   

Sort Numbers by Place Value

Name _____

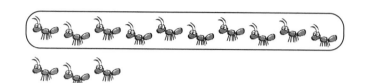

_____1_____ tens _____3_____ ones

How many?_____13_____

_____3_____ tens _____0_____ ones

How many?_____30_____

Circle the objects in sets of ten.

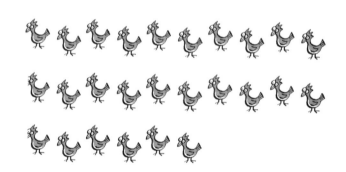

1._____ tens _____ ones

How many?_____

2._____ tens _____ ones

How many?_____

3._____ tens _____ ones

How many?_____

4._____ tens _____ ones

How many?_____

Name _____

___2___ tens ___4___ ones

How many?___24___

___4___ tens ___3___ ones

How many?___43___

How many?

1._____ tens _____ ones

How many?_____

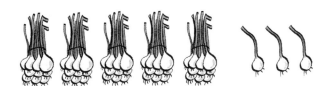

2._____ tens _____ ones

How many?_____

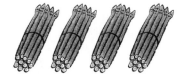

3._____ tens _____ ones

How many?_____

4._____ tens _____ ones

How many?_____

Write the numbers in the chart.

	Tens	Ones
32		
53		
40		
36		

Name _____

Tally Marks

Color in the boxes with even numbers.
Put an **X** in the boxes with odd numbers.
Circle the numbers with zeros.

1	2	3	4	5	6	7	8	9	10
11	12	13	14	15	16	17	18	19	20
21	22	23	24	25	26	27	28	29	30

Tally the numbers on the chart.

	Tally	Number
even		
odd		
zeros		

How many even and odd numbers together? _____

Count from 1 to 50. Tally the even numbers, odd numbers, fives, and tens.

Classify and Graph Numbers

How many even numbers? How many odd numbers?
How many with zeros? Tally the numbers.
Then fill in the bar graph.

22	10	3	25	6	11	26	30	17
13	9	4	14	12	40	7	41	8

	Tally	Number
even		
odd		
with zeros		

Number Graph										
even										
odd										
with zeros										

0 1 2 3 4 5 6 7 8 9 10

Lines of Symmetry

This shape is symmetrical. Both halves are the same.
Some shapes have one line of symmetry.

line of
symmetry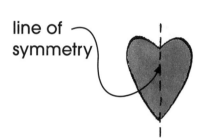

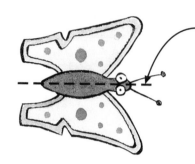 line of
symmetry

Draw the lines of symmetry.

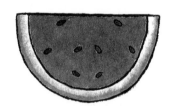

 Draw some shapes, cut them out, and fold them in half to find lines of symmetry. If the two
halves don't match, the shape is not symmetrical.

Lines of Symmetry

Some shapes have two or more lines of symmetry.
Some shapes have no lines of symmetry.

0 lines of symmetry

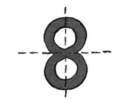

2 lines of symmetry

Many lines of symmetry

Write the number of lines of symmetry under each item.

_____   _____   _____   _____

_____   _____   _____   _____

Fill in the bar graph for the things on this page.

0 lines of symmetry								
1 line of symmetry								
2 or more lines of symmetry								

0   1   2   3   4   5   6   7   8

 Take a hand mirror and cover half of a drawing of a shape. Is the shape symmetrical?
How does the mirror help you see whether something is symmetrical?

     Lines of **Symmetry**

Picture Graphs

This picture graph shows how many books some children in the Bookworms Club read.

Books Read	
Jamie	📗📗📗📗📗📗
Ruth	📗📗📗📗📗📗📗📗📗
Toni	📗📗📗📗📗
Andre	📗📗📗📗📗📗

Each  stands for 5 books.

1. How many books did Toni read? Count by fives. _____

2. Who read the most books? How many did the person read?
_____
_ _ _ _ _ _ _ _ _ _ _ _ _ _ _ _ _ _ _ _
_____ _____

3. Who read as many books as Jamie?
_____
_ _ _ _ _ _ _ _ _ _ _ _ _ _ _ _ _ _ _ _
_____

4. How many books did Ruth and Andre read in all? _____

5. Why do you think the graph has = 5 instead of = 1?

_____
_ _
_____
_ _
_____

Bar Graphs

The table shows how many books Ben, Fran, and Carl read last year.

Books Read	
Ben	卌 卌 卌 卌 卌
Fran	卌 卌 卌 卌 卌 卌
Carl	卌 卌 卌

1. Who read the most books?

_____

- -

_____

2. How many books did the children read all together? _____

3. ✔ the bar graph that matches the table.

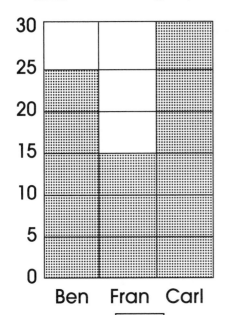

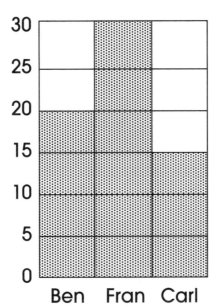

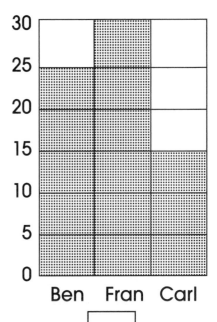

Make a picture graph of the information in the bar graph.
What are the differences between a picture graph and a bar graph?

Picture Graphs

The picture graph shows how many cookies each family ate.

Number of Cookies									
Lopez family	🍪	🍪	🍪	🍪	🍪	🍪	🍪	🍪	
Carter family	🍪	🍪	🍪	🍪	🍪	🍪			
Woo family	🍪	🍪	🍪	🍪	🍪				
Brown family	🍪	🍪	🍪	🍪	🍪	🍪	🍪	🍪	🍪

Each 🍪 stands for 2 cookies.

1. How many cookies did the Carters eat? Count by twos. _____

2. Which family ate the fewest cookies? How many did they eat?

_____

_ _

_____ _____

3. Draw 🍪s in the graph to show that the Woo family ate eight more cookies. What is the family's new total? _____

4. If each person in the Lopez family ate 4 cookies, how many people are in the Lopez family? _____

Bar Graphs

On Arbor Day, some children planted trees in a park. The bar graph shows how many trees of each kind they planted.

Trees Planted on Arbor Day										
apple										
pine										
elm										
	0	5	10	15	20	25	30	35	40	45	50

1. How many apple trees did the children plant? _____

2. How many more pine trees did they plant than elm trees? _____
   _____

   _ _ _ _ _ _ _ _ _ _ _ _ _ _ _ _ _ _

3. Which kind of tree was planted the most? _____

4. How many trees were planted in all? _____

Double Tables

The table shows the rides some children enjoyed.

Ride	Saturday	Sunday
Space Rocket	35	30
Ferris Wheel	50	45
Bumper Cars	20	35
Silver Streak	30	40

1. Which ride had the most riders on Saturday?

_____

_____

2. Which ride had the fewest riders on Sunday?

_____

_____

3. Which ride had ten more riders on Sunday
   than on Saturday?

_____

_____

4. Was the total number of riders greater Saturday or Sunday?

_____

_____

Bar Graphs

Ride	Saturday	Sunday
Space Rocket	35	30
Ferris Wheel	50	45
Bumper Cars	20	35
Silver Streak	30	40

Fill in the bar graphs using the table above.

Riders on Saturday

50
45
40
35
30
25
20
15
10
5
0

Space Rocket	Ferris Wheel	Bumper Cars	Silver Streak

Riders on Sunday

50
45
40
35
30
25
20
15
10
5
0

Space Rocket	Ferris Wheel	Bumper Cars	Silver Streak

 Look at the table and the bar graphs. Which way of presenting information makes it easier to figure out which day had the most visitors?

Coordinate Graphing

Mark a dot for each coordinate pair. Then connect the dots.
Color the picture. The first dot is done for you.

(1,6)
(4,9)
(6,9)
(6,7)
(9,7)
(11,5)
(11,0)
(9,0)
(9,3)
(6,3)
(6,0)
(4,0)
(4,5)

The point (1,6) tells you to move to the right 1 and up 6.

30

Page 1

Page 4

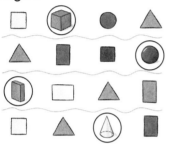

Page 7

Number of Nests

Kyle	🪺 🪺 🪺 🪺 🪺 🪺
Jan	🪺 🪺 🪺
Paco	🪺
Sara	🪺 🪺 🪺

1. Kyle
2. Jan and Sara

Page 10

		Tally Marks	Number
🔵	balls	ⅢⅢ ⅢⅢ	10
🐭	bears	ⅢⅢ ‖	7
🚗	cars	ⅢⅢ ‖	6
🎮	games	ⅢⅢ ‖‖‖	9

Page 12

Coins	Tally Marks	Number
pennies	‖‖‖	4
nickels	‖‖	3
dimes	ⅢⅢ ‖	6
quarters	‖	2

Page 2

Students should sort large bears into one basket, and small bears into the other.

White bears should be sorted into one box, and dark bears into the other.

Page 5

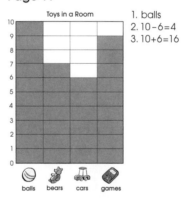

Page 8

1. 10; It rained.
2. 12; It was sunny.
3. cloudy

Page 11

Toys in a Room

1. balls
2. 10 − 6 = 4
3. 10 + 6 = 16

Page 13

Coins in the Bank

	0	1	2	3	4	5	6
pennies							
nickels							
dimes							
quarters							

1. dimes
2. quarters
3. 4 pennies; $0.04
   3 nickels; $0.15
   6 dimes; $0.60
   2 quarters; $0.50
   Total Amount $1.29

Page 3

Page 6

1. 5
2. Sara
3. Jan
4. 11

Page 9

Pets	Votes	
birds	ⅢⅢ	5
dogs	ⅢⅢ ‖‖‖	8
fish	‖‖‖	3
cats	ⅢⅢ ‖‖	7

1. 5
2. 8
3. 3
4. 7
5. dogs

Votes for Favorite Pets

	0	1	2	3	4	5	6	7	8	9	10
birds											
dogs											
fish											
cats											

Page 14

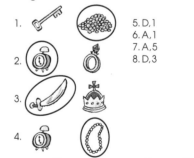

1.
2.
3.
4.

5. D, 1
6. A, 1
7. A, 5
8. D, 3

Page 15

1. C, 6   6. flag
2. D, 1
3. D, 3
4. A, 4
5. D, 4

Page 16

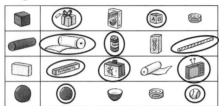

Page 19

1. <u>3</u> tens <u>2</u> ones — <u>32</u>
2. <u>5</u> tens <u>3</u> ones — <u>53</u>
3. <u>4</u> tens <u>0</u> ones — <u>40</u>
4. <u>3</u> tens <u>6</u> ones — <u>36</u>

	Tens	Ones
32	3	2
53	5	3
40	4	0
36	3	6

Page 22

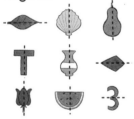

Page 25

1. Fran
2. 70
3.

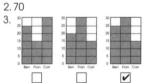

☐ ☐ ☑

Page 28

1. Ferris Wheel
2. Space Rocket
3. Silver Streak
4. Sunday

Page 17

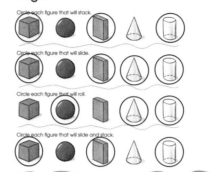

Page 20

	Tally	Number
even	||||| ||||| |||||	15
odd	||||| ||||| |||||	15
zeros	|||	3

30

Page 23

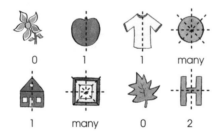

0   1   1   many

1   many   0   2

	0	1	2	3	4	5	6	7	8
0 lines of symmetry									
1 line of symmetry									
2 or more lines of symmetry									

Page 26

1. 12
2. The Woo family; 10
3. Check students' graphs; 18
4. 4

Page 29

Page 18

1. <u>2</u> tens <u>4</u> ones — <u>24</u>
2. <u>2</u> tens <u>6</u> ones — <u>26</u>
3. <u>2</u> tens <u>0</u> ones — <u>20</u>
4. <u>2</u> tens <u>9</u> ones — <u>29</u>

Page 21

	Tally	Number
even	||||| |||||	10
odd	||||| |||	8
with zeros	|||	3

Number Graph											
even											
odd											
with zeros											
	0	1	2	3	4	5	6	7	8	9	10

Page 24

1. 25
2. Ruth; 45
3. Andre
4. 75
5. If the symbol stood for one book, the graph would be too big to read easily.

Page 27

1. 20
2. 5
3. pine
4. 85

Page 30

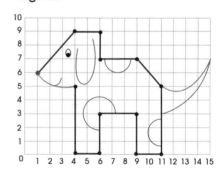

LANGUAGE ARTS 610
Author's Purpose Review

LIFEPAC Test is located in the center of the booklet. Please remove before starting the unit.

Author:
Annis Shepherd

Editor-in-Chief:
Richard W. Wheeler, M.A.Ed.

Editor:
Elizabeth Loeks Bouman

Consulting Editor:
Rudolph Moore, Ph.D.

Revision Editor:
Alan Christopherson, M.S.

MEDIA CREDITS:

Page 6: © Robert Churchill, iStock, Thinkstock; **11:** © scanrail, iStock, Thinkstock; **22:** © Patryk Kosmider, iStock, Thinstock; **26:** © B-C-Designs, iStock, Thinkstock; **42:** © forplayday, iStock, Thinkstock; **45:** © Makkuro_GL, iStock, Thinkstock; **45:** © VectorMine, iStock, Thinkstock.

Alpha Omega
PUBLICATIONS

804 N. 2nd Ave. E.
Rock Rapids, IA 51246-1759

Author's Purpose Review

Introduction

The purpose of this LIFEPAC® is to review the major ideas and skills you learned in the previous nine LIFEPACs this year. The most successful way to review is to put your skills into practice. You are going to be doing much activity in this LIFEPAC, so sharpen your imagination and your pencils, and prepare to enjoy yourself. If you are unsure of any of the skills reviewed in this LIFEPAC, reread the material in the LIFEPAC in which it was taught.

Objectives

Read these objectives. The objectives tell you what you should be able to do when you have successfully completed this LIFEPAC. Each section will list according to the numbers below what objectives will be met in that section. When you have finished the following LIFEPAC, you should be able to:

1. Identify and use a variety of literary forms.

2. Identify the parts of formal and informal letters.

3. Identify the various parts of a newspaper and the contents of each.

4. Edit a mini newspaper.

5. Define advertising.

6. Take notes and organize them.

7. Describe and use the various elements of a story.

8. Write a short story and an essay.

9. Identify and use sources of information.

10. Identify sentence patterns and apply grammatical rules.

11. Identify and apply the rules of punctuation.

12. Identify and apply common spelling patterns.

13. Identify vowel digraphs, homonyms, antonyms, and synonyms.

14. Apply various handwriting skills.

Survey the LIFEPAC. Ask yourself some questions about this study and write your questions here.

_____

_____

_____

_____

_____

_____

_____

_____

_____

_____

_____

_____

_____

_____

_____

_____

_____

_____

_____

_____

1. SECTION ONE

In Section One, you will review the many methods of communication. You will explore the use of persuasive words in advertising, design you own book cover and advertisement, plan your final LIFEPAC project (which is to edit a mini newspaper), and participate in various types of letter-writing skills. You will also review spelling skills and handwriting techniques.

Section Objectives

Review these objectives. When you have completed this section, you should be able to:

1. Identify and use a variety of literary forms.
2. Identify the parts of formal and informal letters.
3. Identify the various parts of a newspaper and the contents of each.
4. Edit a mini newspaper.
5. Define advertising.
12. Identify and apply common spelling patterns.
14. Apply various handwriting skills.

Vocabulary

Study these words to enhance your learning success in this section.

aspiration (as pu rā shun). A strong wish or aim.

benefactor (ben u fak tur). One who confers a benefit.

facet (fas it). An aspect of a topic.

gesture (jes chur). The use of movement of the limbs or body as a means of expression.

grimace (gru mās). A twist of the face expressing disapproval.

motivate (mō tu vā t). To stir to action.

ornate (ôr nāt). Much decorated.

overlap (ō vur lap). To go over and beyond a barrier.

persuasive (pur swā siv). Influencing the mind by arguments and reasons.

propaganda (prop u gan du). An organized effort to spread a particular point of view.

reassuring (rē u shūr ing). To restore confidence.

symbol (sim bul). A sign that stands for something else.

technique (tek nēk). The method or the details of procedure essential to expertness in an art or science.

verbally (vėr bu lē). To do with words; pertaining to words.

Note: *All vocabulary words in this LIFEPAC appear in* **boldface** *print the first time they are used. If you are unsure of the meaning when you are reading, study the definitions given.*

Pronunciation Key: hat, āge, cãre, fär; let, ēqual, tėrm; it, īce; hot, ōpen, ôrder; oil; out; cup, put, rüle; child; long; thin; /ŦH/ for then; /zh/ for measure; /u/ or /ə/ represents /a/ in about, /e/ in taken, /i/ in pencil, /o/ in lemon, and /u/ in circus.

COMMUNICATION AND ITS PURPOSES

Communication is used by humans to exchange information—all kinds of information. This exchange takes place in the form of **symbols**—mathematical symbols, musical symbols, verbal symbols, and even body language (**grimaces**, **gestures**, etc.).

We communicate **verbally** through speech; also through letters, books, poetry, advertisements, newspapers, text messaging, social media, and web pages.

Books and poetry are forms of entertainment and instruction. Advertisements are a form of **propaganda**, and are often used to try to control or motivate our behavior. For example, when a person buys a can of beans, he often selects the can with the most attractive label or the most catchy name. Newspapers and reports give us information. Letters, both formal and informal, express our feelings and ideas.

Many of these types of communication can **overlap**. For example, books and poetry and even songs can be used as propaganda. Letters can be a form of entertainment. In fact, a book can be written in the form of letters. Many early novels were written in this style. The amusing book *Daddy Long Legs* by Jean Webster was written this way. It tells the story of an orphan girl who is sent to college by an unknown **benefactor**. She calls him Daddy Long Legs because all she saw of him was his gigantic shadow which resembled a spider.

In this LIFEPAC you will be expected to communicate, using the **techniques** of expression you have learned throughout the year.

Advertising. Effective advertising contains specially selected words which help persuade you, the buyer, to choose a certain article. These words are called **persuasive** words. Persuasive words make the buyer think he is not only getting a bargain but is getting the best.

For example, "It provides steady, continuous, effective chlorination," contains three **reassuring** adjectives. Interesting titles and "catchy" expressions also can be persuasive. Illustrations say more if they are not too **ornate**.

Rearrange and number the ideas in the correct sequence, as they appeared in the previous paragraphs.

1.1 _____ Newspapers and reports give us information.

1.2 _____ Many early novels were written as a series of letters.

1.3 _____ Advertising is a form of propaganda.

1.4 _____ *Daddy Long Legs* was written as a series of letters.

1.5 _____ Exchange of information takes place in the form of symbols.

1.6 _____ Letters express our feelings and ideas.

1.7 _____ Many of these types of communication can overlap.

Answer this question.

1.8 Which of the statements in the last activity expresses the main idea about communication?

_____

Complete this activity.

1.9 Separate the persuasive words from the following list of words and place them on the lines.

flowers	scientifically balanced	professional
guest	greenhouse	transmission
luscious	real bargain	machine
bigger	hammer	improved
extremely	savings	unique
earth	recommended	fantastic
healthier	weather	food

a. _____   b. _____   c. _____

d. _____   e. _____   f. _____

g. _____   h. _____   i. _____

j. _____   k. _____   l. _____

Match the following cliché metaphors with their meanings. Use the internet to help if you have any difficulty.

1.10 _____ eat humble pie; served a slice of humble pie

1.11 _____ eat one's heart out

1.12 _____ eat one's words

1.13 _____ eat like a horse

1.14 _____ bite off more than you can chew

1.15 _____ wolf down food

a. to withdraw what you have said

b. to take on more than you can handle

c. to eat a home-cooked meal

d. to eat tremendous amounts of food

e. to eat very quickly

f. to be dejected or unhappy

g. to beg for forgiveness in a very humble way

Make up your own advertisement.

1.16 Illustrate, color, and design your advertisement on another sheet of paper. Remember to have catchy titles, persuasive words, and simple (but attractive) illustrations. Look at as many sources as possible and notice the variety of styles used in advertisements before starting your own. You may cut out parts of pictures and reassemble them in such a way to create a new picture in the form of a collage. Ask a friend for their opinion about your advertisement. Get your advertisement ready for your mini newspaper.

Friend's name _____

Design a book jacket!

1.17 Design a dust jacket (book cover) that will catch the buyer's or reader's eye. You may use the jacket as an advertisement for a book in your mini newspaper.

Helpful Hints
- First, look at as many book covers as you can.
- Decide what kind of border to have.
- Decide how large and what shape your title will be.
- Decide where to place your title and in what direction it will go.
- Decide the color scheme—does it fit the topic?

TEACHER CHECK _____ _____
initials   date

Letter writing. You can write letters either for pleasure, to tell news, to apply for a job, to tell someone your **aspirations**, to invite someone to a party, to thank someone, or to obtain information. Whatever your reason for writing, you must communicate your thoughts and feelings in the simplest and clearest manner to avoid misunderstanding. Formal letters are written to people you do not know well. You keep a formal letter short and to the point, and make it polite rather than chatty. Informal letters are written to people you know well enough to call by their first name. The tone of informal letters is friendly.

Complete these activities.

1.18 Indicate the kind of letters you would write to the following people. Write *I* for informal and *F* for formal on the line.

a. _____ doctor

b. _____ pastor

c. _____ your brother

d. _____ principal

e. _____ Aunt Mary

f. _____ a cousin

g. _____ senator

h. _____ bank president

i. _____ a pen pal

j. _____ editor of a newspaper

k. _____ your mother

l. _____ the mayor

1.19 Write three formal greetings and closings.

Greetings:

a. _____

b. _____

c. _____

Closings:

d. _____

e. _____

f. _____

1.20 Write three informal greetings and closings.

Greetings:

a. _____

b. _____

c. _____

Closings:

d. _____

e. _____

f. _____

1.21 Write a letter to the editor for your mini newspaper.

TEACHER CHECK _____ _____

initials   date

Write a letter to yourself.

1.22 Write a private letter to yourself to be opened in five or ten years' time. Write down the way you see yourself as a person, and note your aspirations for the future. Seal it and give it to your parents to keep safely for you. You will be interested to see how you will feel, and maybe how you have changed when you open it.

PARENT CHECK

_____ _____
initials   date

Newspapers. Newspapers have many communication purposes. Newspapers can inform, entertain, and persuade. They can help to bring people together, to raise funds, to expose the truth, and to advertise. An important **facet** of journalistic writing is simplicity. Facts are required, not opinions. Some newspaper writers allow their opinions and prejudices to show through their writing, which can be a form of propaganda. Opinions belong only on the editorial page.

Match the following newspaper sections with their contents.

1.23 _____ house for rent for summer only

1.24 _____ Earthquake Shatters New York Skyscrapers

1.25 _____ a letter attacking newspaper policy

1.26 _____ a death announcement

1.27 _____ Rose Bowl game

1.28 _____ a local parade and pageant

a. obituaries

b. entertainment

c. weather

d. sports

e. classified ads

f. editorial page

g. front page

CREATIVE PROJECT

This project will bring together all the skills and literary forms you have studied this year. In order to enjoy this activity and to get as much value from it as possible, you should

1. use your imagination,

2. aim for high quality of craftsmanship, and

3. make something that you can be pleased with.

You will create a mini newspaper. Your newspaper should consist of six (or more) regular school sheets of blank paper. Either staple or tape the middle sections together. The following newspaper section should be included; front page, editorial page, weather, obituaries, sports page, advertisements, classified ads, entertainment, short story and poetry competitions, crossword puzzles, cartoons, recipes, question and answer column, and religion section. Work hard on this project for the next couple of weeks. Your teacher will check it when you have finished this LIFEPAC.

Helpful Hints

- Look at any newspaper and see how it is set up.

- Choose your title for your newspaper.

- When writing your lead articles, use your friends or storybook characters as the basis of articles, such as *Red Riding Hood Has the Mumps—Wolf Panics!*

- You may include pictures from magazines and newspapers but make up your own titles and comments.

- The important thing is be inventive! Use propaganda techniques and catch your reader's eye.

- Remember to use the tall-tale story technique when writing some of your articles.

Complete this activity.

1.29 Write the sections you plan to have in your newspaper. After each one, write suggestions for articles, pictures, headlines, and so forth.

a. _____

   _____

b. _____

   _____

c. _____

   _____

d. _____

   _____

e. _____

   _____

f. _____

   _____

TEACHER CHECK _____ _____
                     initials   date

SPELLING AND HANDWRITING

Your spelling words were taken from Language Arts LIFEPAC 601 and 602. Your handwriting will review hints for fluency in cursive writing.

Spelling. Remember, recognizing patterns in words helps you with the spelling. Notice that the first two columns contain homonyms. Notice that the second two columns contain different ways of spelling the sound of /sh/.

Review or relearn the spelling words in Spelling Words-1.

SPELLING WORDS-1

Review Words-601

pursuit	thievery	boardwalk
disease	relieve	amethyst
treaty	receipt	mosquito
jealous	yielded	pamphlet
treacherous	leisure	penguin
disguise	acquaint	licorice
guidance	Wednesday	etiquette

Review Words-602

ascend	existence	conscience
gracious	dependent	version
responsible	accomplish	authority
commercial	civilization	commission
achieve	presence	opportunity
artificial	missionary	appreciate
association	tradition	enthusiastic

Complete this activity.

1.30 Copy the Review Words-602 Spelling Words in your best handwriting, placing them all in alphabetical order.

a. _____   b. _____   c. _____

d. _____   e. _____   f. _____

g. _____   h. _____   i. _____

j. _____   k. _____   l. _____

m. _____   n. _____   o. _____

p. _____   q. _____   r. _____

s. _____   t. _____   u. _____

Find the eleven Review Words-602 Spelling Words that have the sound of /*sh*/ but are not spelled with *sh*.

1.31 Write the words on these lines.

a. _____   b. _____   c. _____

d. _____   e. _____   f. _____

g. _____   h. _____   i. _____

j. _____   k. _____

Hunt the words. Use your detective powers and find the hidden words in the first paragraph of the introductory discussion "Communication and Its Purposes" on page 6. The hidden word may be part of one or two words. Write the word(s) from the paragraph and circle the hidden word. You will be given a clue.

Example: Clue: snooze <u>when a person</u> _____

1.32 Clue: a musical sound _____

1.33 Clue: part of a foot _____

1.34 Clue: to suspend _____

1.35 Clue: a floor covering _____

1.36 Clue: part of a fish _____

1.37 Clue: opposite of hers _____

1.38 Clue: obtain _____

1.39 Clue: a kind of trimming _____

1.40 Clue: not youth _____

1.41 Clue: found on the seashore _____

1.42 Clue: edge _____

1.43 Clue: a spice made from a nutmeg shell _____

1.44 Clue: replace _____

Test your word skills. Complete the puzzle.

1.45 Add one letter each time to the previous word and form a new word.

Example: it, sit, slit, split, splint, splints

Follow the clues to help you.

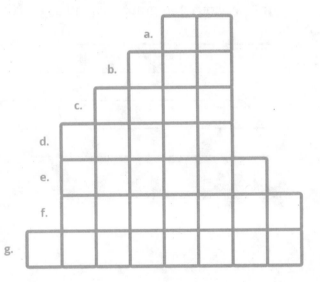

a. Clue: A preposition rhyming with *hat*

b. Clue: gobbled

c. Clue: tardy

d. Clue: a dish

e. Clue: name of an American river

f. Clue: a large dish

g. Clue: to sprinkle or dot something

Make a similar word puzzle of your own.

1.46 Make your own puzzle on an extra sheet of paper and try it on one of your friends. Include it in your mini newspaper.

Friend's name _____

ABC   **Ask your teacher to give you a practice spelling test of Spelling Words-1.** Restudy the words you missed.

Handwriting. To gain fluency and speed in your handwriting, remember to:

1) hold your pencil fairly loosely, not tightly;
2) press lightly, not hard;
3) hold your book at an angle; and
4) let the pencil point away from you at an angle, not straight up vertically.

Copy a proverb.

1.47 Select a two-line proverb from the Bible and copy it twice on these lines. Keep the points from the previous paragraph in mind as you do so, and aim at speed as well as attractiveness.

_____

_____

_____

_____

_____

TEACHER CHECK _____ _____

initials   date

Review the material in this section in preparation for the Self Test. This Self Test will check your mastery of this particular section. The items missed on this Self Test will indicate specific areas where restudy is needed for mastery.

SELF TEST 1

Match these items by writing the correct letter in the blank (each answer, 2 points).

1.01	_____ a book written in the form of a series of letters	a. dust jacket
1.02	_____ a section of the newspaper that announces funerals	b. grimace
1.03	_____ the opening line of a letter	c. classified ads
1.04	_____ the last words of a letter	d. to persuade
1.05	_____ the paper cover of a book	e. propaganda
1.06	_____ a metaphor	f. formal
1.07	_____ a form of communication used to persuade	g. obituaries
1.08	_____ body language	h. eat dirt
1.09	_____ the tone of a business letter	i. *Daddy Long Legs*
1.010	_____ the purpose of advertising	j. closing
		k. greeting

Complete these statements (each answer, 3 points).

1.011 Communication is used by humans to exchange _____ .

1.012 An important characteristic of journalistic writing is _____ .

1.013 Personal letters are not formal, they are _____ .

1.014 Newspaper articles usually contain _____ , not opinions.

1.015 The aim of persuasion is to motivate or change _____ .

1.016 Words like *reliable, effective, long-lasting* are _____ words.

1.017 A letter to an editor would be a(n) _____ letter.

1.018 In a newspaper, opinions belong only on the _____ page.

Complete this list (each item, 3 points).

1.019 List six major sections of a newspaper.

a. _____   b. _____

c. _____   d. _____

e. _____   f. _____

Complete this list (each item, 2 points).

1.020 List three purposes of a newspaper.

a. _____

b. _____

c. _____

Answer true or false (each answer, 2 points).

1.021 _____ Poetry is a form of verbal communication.

1.022 _____ Propaganda makes everybody buy things.

1.023 _____ We can express our feelings and ideas in informal letters.

1.024 _____ Body language is a form of communication.

1.025 _____ All early novels were written in the form of letters.

1.026 _____ Exchange of information takes place in the form of symbols.

1.027 _____ Persuasive words are necessary in effective advertising.

1.028 _____ Pressing down too hard with your pencil can speed up your writing.

1.029 _____ Body language means using either your hands or your feet to write with.

1.030 _____ Words are verbal symbols.

Write the definition of these terms (each answer, 3 points).

1.031 cliché: _____

_____

1.032 persuasive words: _____

_____

1.033 classified ads: _____

_____

1.034 advertising: _____

_____

80 / 100	SCORE _____	TEACHER _____ _____
		initials date

ABC **Take your spelling test of Spelling Words-1.**

2. SECTION TWO

You will review the various literary forms you have studied this year. You have studied the areas of fiction, prose, nonfiction, poetry, and other styles of literary communication.

Now you will put some of these literary forms into practice. You will further improve your spelling skills and handwriting fluency and also review homonyms, synonyms, and antonyms.

Section Objectives

Review these objectives. When you have completed this section, you should be able to:

1. Identify and use a variety of literary forms.
7. Describe and use the various elements of a story.
8. Write a short story and an essay.
9. Identify and use sources of information.
13. Identify vowel digraphs, homonyms, antonyms, and synonyms.
14. Apply various handwriting skills.

Vocabulary

Study these words to enhance your learning success in this section.

category (kat u gõr ē). A class or division of classification.

incident (in su dunt). Event or occurrence that takes place.

instructive (in struk tiv). Conveying or giving knowledge.

manipulate (mu nip yu lāt). To control the action by management.

numerous (nū mur us). A great number.

version (vėr zhun). An account or description from a particular point of view.

Pronunciation Key: hat, āge, cãre, fär; let, ēqual, tėrm; it, īce; hot, ōpen, ôrder; oil; out; cup, put, rüle; child; long; thin; /ŦH/ for then; /zh/ for measure; /u/ or /ə/ represents /a/ in about, /e/ in taken, /i/ in pencil, /o/ in lemon, and /u/ in circus.

LITERARY FORMS

Verbal communication is expressed in many literary styles. In Section One you reviewed the literary forms of the newspaper, advertisements, and book jackets. These forms are only three of a long list of stylistic forms. Fairy tales, legends, myths, tall tales, and fables are very old literary forms. For instance, the earliest **version** of the familiar fairy tale "Cinderella" found anywhere in the world occurs in a Chinese book written about A.D. 850 to 860. In this story the Chinese Cinderella was called Yeh-hsien, and instead of a glass slipper, she had a gold shoe. Fables, imaginary stories that use talking animals to teach lessons, and tall tales, exaggerated stories about the wonderful deeds of a hero, are literary forms which go back hundreds of years. As for the form of the myth, it goes back thousands of years. Novels and short stories as we know them today are much more recent literary forms.

The term *poetry* covers a large number of forms of styles, from long ballads to short, two-line poems or couplets. As for the variety of forms used in the area of nonfiction, they are so **numerous** that they will be covered separately later in this LIFEPAC.

As with any skill, whether it be in the musical, sports, business, or physical-labor areas, you need practice in order to be good at it. **Manipulating** words is a very difficult skill, but with much practice you can learn to write and create skillfully. You do need imagination and enthusiasm, but only you can cultivate these characteristics in your work. Try to do so as you proceed with this LIFEPAC.

Rearrange and number the ideas in the correct sequence, as they appeared in the previous paragraphs.

2.1 _____ The form of the myth goes back thousands of years.

2.2 _____ With much practice you can learn to write and create skillfully.

2.3 _____ Fairy tales, legends, and myths are very old literary forms.

2.4 _____ The term *poetry* covers a large number of forms or styles.

2.5 _____ Verbal communication is expressed in many literary styles.

2.6 _____ Novels and short stories are much more recent literary forms.

2.7 _____ Manipulating words is a very difficult skill.

Answer this question.

2.8 Which of the statements in Activities 2.1- 2.7 expresses the main idea about literary forms?

_____

Complete the following word play.

2.9 Unscramble the following literary forms.

a. ngsedel   _____

b. royetp   _____

c. bsealf   _____

d. sysaes   _____

e. vlsneo   _____

f. hystm   _____

g. arnluojs   _____

h. ltla elsat   _____

Fiction. The term *fiction* includes all written stories which are based on untrue **incidents** or characters. The main purpose of fiction is to entertain, although it can also be **instructive** and contain some true or factual information.

Legends, fables, tall tales, fairy tales, myths, novels, and short stories all come under the **category** of fiction. Novels are the longest form, and are usually separated into chapters. Short novels are either called novellas or novelettes depending on the number of words they have. In a novel, the reader follows the lives and activities of many characters over a fairly long period of time. A short story usually deals with one major character and the plot covers a short space of time.

Because of the length of the short story, it is necessary to concentrate on one major theme or action—in other words, the writer must keep to one point of view and not ramble on. They must choose his words carefully (like a poet) and say a lot in a few words.

In the following exercise remember to keep the basic elements of a story in mind: exposition (characters and setting), conflict, rising action, climax, falling action, and resolution. Plunge right into the middle of your action and gradually lay bare your problem and setting as your action builds to a climax. You will first build your vocabulary so that you can make your story more exciting.

Nonfiction. Nonfiction includes all textbooks, magazine articles, autobiographies, biographies, journals, and essays that are based on fact and give information. If any of these forms includes more opinion than fact, it is less accurate. The reader must be able to separate fact from opinion in order to learn the truth about the world around them.

 Complete these activities.

2.10 These words beginning with *e* could describe the action and situation shown in the picture. Find their meanings in the dictionary if you do not know them.

edible	expire	embarrassed	exist
exasperated	electric	exhausted	endure
expand	express	encrusted	exciting

2.11 Explore your dictionary for more adjectives, adverbs, nouns, and verbs beginning with *e* that could be used when writing a story about the picture. Write these words on the lines.

_____

_____

_____

_____

_____

_____

TEACHER CHECK _____ _____

initials   date

Write a story with words beginning with e. Use as many vivid adjectives beginning with *e* as you can.

2.12 Write a story on an extra sheet of paper about the picture of the fish, using a minimum of thirty words beginning with the letter *e*. Underline all the *e* words in your story. For example, "The *electric* fish had a jewel-*encrusted* back which sparkled in the *emerald* green waves." Try to imagine what the man in the water is doing or searching for; what is causing such excitement among these fantastic sharks. Is the man a heroic character and the sharks the enemy, or the reverse? Explore the motives behind the characters in your story and describe the setting and mood of your story in a colorful and interesting way. This story can go into your mini newspaper.

TEACHER CHECK _____ _____
                        initials   date

Complete this activity.

2.13 Label each story by putting its literary form in the blank provided.

    a. _____ "Cinderella"

    b. _____ *The Giver*

    c. _____ "The Hare and the Tortoise"

    d. _____ "How Atlas Was Made to Hold Up the World"

    e. _____ "Paul Bunyan," "Johnny Appleseed"

    f. _____ "Robin Hood and His Merry Men"

    g. _____ "Sleeping Beauty"

Indicate on the blanks provided whether the statements are facts or opinions. Write an *F* if it is a fact and an *O* if it is an opinion.

2.14 _____ The island of Corsica is in the Mediterranean Sea.

2.15 _____ Children have an incredible amount of energy.

2.16 _____ Pineapples mixed with pears make a delightful drink.

2.17 _____ The number of accidents on the roads in Arizona has increased over the past three years according to traffic records.

2.18 _____ Baseball is a more fascinating game than football.

2.19 _____ The Olympic Games are a means of bringing members of opposing countries together peacefully.

2.20 _____ Pink is a more attractive color than orange.

Write a short essay of no more than ten lines on the "Advantages of Having Green Hair."
Remember to pack in as much information as you can in the fewest, most interesting, number of
words. This essay can be copied on a separate sheet of paper and used as a feature article in the
Entertainment Section of your mini newspaper.

2.21 _____

_____

_____

_____

_____

_____

_____

_____

_____

_____

_____

_____

TEACHER CHECK _____ _____
                          initials   date

Complete the following activity.

2.22 Imagine that you have just received the news that you have been elected President of the
United States. You have decided to record your feelings in your journal or diary. On an extra
sheet of paper, write down the feelings you think you would have on such an occasion.
Remember, because it is a journal, you will be writing in the first person or "I" form.
Write as if it is happening to you right now. This writing can be a feature article in your mini
newspaper if you wish.

TEACHER CHECK _____ _____
                          initials   date

Poetry. As you learned in Language Arts LIFEPAC 606, poetry comes in all shapes and sizes. Free verse, ballads, limericks, cinquains, and haiku are only a few of the different ways a poem can be written.
A collection of poetry is called an **anthology**.

Poetry sounds different from prose because of the musical and rhythmical way the poet has combined his words. Many ideas and feelings are expressed in only a few lines. One way a poet is able to give his statements a musical quality is to use repetition, either of words, sounds, or letters.

Here are two examples showing repetition:

a. The grass was green, greener than the underside of a frog.

b. Each leaf, mist-moistened, mirrored the magic of the sun.

In Example b., not only is the sound of *m* repeated, but so are the short vowel *i* and the letter *s*, all combining to give a dreamy quality to the image.

Make up three of your own "Musical One-Liners" by using repetition of either sounds, words, or letters.

2.23 Write your "Musical One-Liners" on the lines.

a. _____

b. _____

c. _____

Bible literary forms. Bible literary forms are like other literary forms in some ways but different in other ways. Many true short stories are found in the Bible, but most of them are interwoven with Bible history. Esther is the only short story that has a separate book. Parables are very short stories that teach special lessons. The New Testament parables always have spiritual meanings that unbelievers do not see.

Proverbs are short, wise sayings. Proverbs are a kind of Hebrew verse in that proverbs use the poetic device of parallelism. The language and subject matter of proverbs, however, is not like true poetry. True Hebrew poetry is found in greatest quantity in the book of Psalms. Poetry is found in many other parts of the Bible, as well.

Hebrew poetry does not rhyme, but it does have cadence. Many of the psalms were written as songs of worship. The subject matter, language, and emotional tone of Hebrew poetry is usually lofty and intense. The poetic device of parallelism is characteristic of Hebrew poetry. Two or more sentences or parts of sentences balance each other. Sometimes the balance is made by restating the first sentence in other words. Sometimes the second sentence starts the same as the first sentence but is changed in the last part. Sometimes the second part is a contrast to the first. Poetic prose is found throughout both the Old Testament and the New Testament.

As a literary form, prophetic writing is unique to the Bible. Within the prophetic writings are to be found stories, parables, history, and biography. Prophecy was usually written in poetry or poetic prose.

Prophecy was often in the form of sermons about what the Israelites should do. Prophecy also told many things that would happen in the future.

The first five books of the Bible are sometimes classified as history but are usually called *The Law*. Most of Leviticus and Deuteronomy and much of Exodus and Numbers are concerned with The Law. The basic law is contained in the Ten Commandments, which are recorded in Exodus 20:1–17. Ceremonial law and health and welfare laws make up the rest. The Law was written in a precise and orderly fashion called a code.

History and biography are interwoven in the Bible. Incidental history is told in many of the books of the Bible. God caused the prophets to interpret history to the Israelites. New Testament history is the record of Jesus, God's Son, coming to earth to provide salvation for men. The book of Acts is the history of the early church.

If anything about Bible literary forms does not come quickly to your mind, reread the sections in Language Arts LIFEPAC 609.

Match these words and phrases.

2.24 _____ the purpose for which many of the Psalms were written

2.25 _____ unique to the Bible as a literary form

2.26 _____ usually interwoven with Bible history

2.27 _____ the form in which the Mosaic Law was written

2.28 _____ very short stories that teach lessons

2.29 _____ the only Biblical short story that is a separate book

2.30 _____ the passage in which the Ten Commandments are found

2.31 _____ the four Gospels and Acts

2.32 _____ these always have hidden spiritual meanings

a. New Testament parables

b. to be sung in worship

c. a code

d. Esther

e. proverbs

f. parables

g. biography

h. Exodus 20:1-17

i. New Testament history

j. example of parallelism

k. Biblical prophecy

Special literary forms. Many types of books do not really fit into either fiction, nonfiction, or poetry categories.

These books are:

1) periodicals (which can contain fact, fiction, and/or opinion);
2) dictionaries, encyclopedias, almanacs, *Who's Who*, atlas;
3) a thesaurus; and
4) a concordance.

Many of these books aid you in gathering or locating information.
Two other techniques that are used in literary exercises are the interview and photography.

 Complete this activity.

2.33 Look in a standard dictionary and find the meaning of the following terms.

a. one-shot _____

b. one-track _____

c. one-two _____

d. one-up _____

e. one-sided _____

f. one-liner _____

Complete the following "Family Description Tree." Remember to use the interview technique to find information regarding dates and places. You might like to attach small photographs to your chart to make your information even more accurate.

2.34 Fill in your "Family Description Tree." Use as many adjectives and phrases as you can to describe each member of your family and place them in the boxes.

YOUR FATHER'S PARENTS

Your Grandfather

Name _____

Born _____

Where _____

Your Grandmother

Name _____

Born _____

Where _____

Name _____

Your
father married
Date _____

Born _____

Where _____

(Place information for yourself and your siblings in the boxes below.)

Name _____

Born _____

Name _____

Born _____

Name _____

Born _____

Use adjectives that describe their characters, their attitudes and their appearance. For example, sympathetic, understanding, humorous, or frank. Interview your parents and grandparents for information.

YOUR MOTHER'S PARENTS

Your Grandfather

Name _____

Born _____

Where _____

Your Grandmother

Name _____

Born _____

Where _____

Name _____

Your mother

Born _____

Where _____

(Place information for yourself and your siblings in the boxes below.)

Name _____

Born _____

Name _____

Born _____

Name _____

Born _____

PARENT CHECK _____ _____
initials   date

SPELLING AND HANDWRITING

Your spelling words were taken from Language Arts LIFEPACs 603 and 604. Your handwriting will review difficult joinings of certain letters.

Spelling. Your spelling words include words containing the digraphs *ie*, *ea*, *oa*, and *ee*. They also include antonyms and words with negative prefixes.

Review or learn the spelling of the words in Spelling Words-2.

SPELLING WORDS-2

Review Words-603

believe	defeat	legible
proceed	leather	between
toadstool	soldier	deceit
release	railroad	oatmeal
breakfast	reveal	receive
conceit	achieve	boatswain
eerie	headache	either

Review Words-604

ascend	combine	beautiful
responsible	immediately	thoughtful
occupied	lose	impractical
dependable	barren	separate
incomplete	acquire	decline
accept	unreasonable	unfinished
vacant	fertile	descend

Complete these activities from the LIFEPAC 603 Spelling Words.

2.35 List the four spelling words with the vowel digraph *ie*.

a. _____   b. _____

c. _____   d. _____

2.36 List the four spelling words with the vowel digraph *oa*.

a. _____   b. _____

c. _____   d. _____

2.37 List the three spelling words whose vowel digraph *ea* has the sound of long *e*.

a. _____   b. _____   c. _____

2.38 List the three spelling words whose vowel digraph *ea* has the sound of short *e*.

a. _____   b. _____   c. _____

2.39 List the three spelling words that follow the rule of *i before e except after c*.

a. _____   b. _____   c. _____

Complete this activity using Review Words-604 Spelling Words.

2.40 List the six pairs of antonyms (words that have opposite meanings).

a. _____   b. _____   c. _____

_____   _____   _____

d. _____   e. _____   f. _____

_____   _____   _____

Fill in the blanks using any of the following pairs of homonyms.

current	assent	taught	dessert
hoarse	altar	currant	horse
desert	taut	ascent	alter

2.41 The man on the a. _____ had a b. _____ voice.

2.42 The church decided not to a. _____ the size of their

b. _____ for the new building.

2.43 Rather than a. _____ the group, the man ate chicken and

b. _____ .

2.44 The leader gave his a. _____ to the men making an

b. _____ on Mount Everest.

2.45 The sailor had been a. _____ to pull all the ship's ropes

b. _____ .

2.46 The magic a. _____ got caught by the b. _____ and was

swept down the river.

Match the words with their synonyms.

2.47 _____ ignorant

2.48 _____ thoughtful

2.49 _____ feed

2.50 _____ conceal

2.51 _____ specimen

2.52 _____ stumble

2.53 _____ inattentive

2.54 _____ breeze

2.55 _____ peaceful

2.56 _____ stern

a. nourish

b. draught

c. grim

d. superstitious

e. restful

f. untaught

g. considerate

h. hide

i. sample

j. unmindful

k. trip

ABC **Ask your teacher to give you a practice spelling test of Spelling Words-2.** Restudy the words you missed.

Handwriting. Certain joinings of letters are difficult in cursive writing. These joinings usually involve the letter *r* when it follows any letter whose flourish or tail is at the top of the letter rather than at the bottom.

> Example: *br, vr, wr*

Practice the following letter combinations. Make sure that the joining loops dip slightly before the *r* is formed.

2.57

br   or   vr   wr

Review the material in this section to prepare for the Self Test. This Self Test will check your understanding of this section and will review the first section. Any items you miss in this test will show you what areas you need to restudy.

SELF TEST 2

Write six literary forms that come under the heading of *fiction* (each answer, 3 points).

2.01 _____

2.02 _____

2.03 _____

2.04 _____

2.05 _____

2.06 _____

Complete this matching exercise. Write the letter of the source you would use to find the following information (each answer, 2 points).

2.07 _____ an interview with the current US president

2.08 _____ the meaning of the word *fluency*

2.09 _____ the background and history of Martin Luther King

2.010 _____ the state bird of Montana

2.011 _____ the synonyms of the word *eat*

2.012 _____ the position of the Canary Islands

2.013 _____ the poems of Robert Louis Stevenson

2.014 _____ the times of the sunset and the sunrise on January 6, 2010

2.015 _____ an alphabetical list of words in a book with the passages where they are found

a. anthology

b. concordance

c. a thesaurus

d. a periodical

e. essay

f. almanac

g. dictionary

h. atlas

i. encyclopedia

j. *Who's Who*

LANGUAGE ARTS 610

LIFEPAC TEST

NAME _____

DATE _____

SCORE _____

LANGUAGE ARTS 610: LIFEPAC TEST

Write the nouns and verbs from each sentence (each answer, 1 point).

1. The aged emperor bowed his grey head and prayed.

   Nouns (2)   a. _____   b. _____

   Verbs (2)   c. _____   d. _____

2. A whale spouts water from a hole in its head.

   Nouns (4)   a. _____   b. _____

                          c. _____   d. _____

   Verbs (1)   e. _____

Write the adjectives and adverbs from the following sentences (each answer, 1 point). Do not repeat words.

3. The sly old fox jumped quickly into the square box.

   Adjectives (4)   a. _____   b. _____

                              c. _____   d. _____

   Adverbs (1)   e. _____

4. Tasty cheese crackers with green onion dip sat deliciously on the table.

   Adjectives (4)   a. _____   b. _____

                              c. _____   d. _____

   Adverbs (1)   e. _____

Write the pronouns and helping (auxiliary) verbs in the following sentences (each answer, 1 point).

5. Bill said you would come with me.

   Pronouns (2)   a. _____   b. _____

   Auxiliary verb (1)   c. _____

6. Sally, her mother, and I are going to the fair.

   Pronoun (1)   a. _____

   Auxiliary verb (1)   b. _____

Match the following terms with their examples (each answer, 2 points).

7. _____ green with envy

8. _____ has a formal greeting

9. _____ uses persuasive words

10. _____ techniques used to change and control people's opinions

11. _____ to find different words that mean the same or the opposite

12. _____ has an informal closing

13. _____ an exclamation mark

14. _____ describe verbs, adjectives, or adverbs

15. _____ contains facts

16. _____ may contain both fact and opinion

a. propaganda

b. letter to a friend

c. cliché metaphor

d. metaphor

e. advertisement

f. nonfiction

g. adverbs

h. business letter

i. punctuation

j. thesaurus

k. editorial

Complete these statements (each answer, 3 points).

17. A story about the wonderful deeds of a hero is a _____ .

18. An imaginary story that uses talking animals to teach lessons is a _____ .

19. A collection of writings of one kind or from one country or century is an _____ .

20. A book of short biographies of famous people is _____ .

21. A very short teaching story from the Bible is a _____ .

22. Balancing phrases or sentences is called _____ .

23. Poetry must have rhythm or cadence but not necessarily _____ .

24. A literary form found only in the Bible is _____ .

Write these notes under the correct subheadings (each answer, 2 points).

Four thousand people fed	A few small fishes	Seven loaves of bread
Seven baskets full left over	No food for three days	Four thousand hungry people

A Miracle of Supply

I. The Need

25. A. _____

26. B. _____

II. The Supply

27. A. _____

28. B. _____

III. The Results

29. A. _____

30. B. _____

Answer true or false (each answer, 2 points).

31. _____ *Up* and *down* are synonyms.

32. _____ The characters and the problem they have are at the center of every story.

33. _____ The setting of a story is the place where the story happens.

34. _____ The headline "Egypt and Israel Sign Peace Treaty" belongs on the sports page.

35. _____ The climax of a story is in the introduction.

36. _____ *Hair* and *hare* are among homonyms.

37. _____ The headline "Grace Academy Takes All-City Championship" belongs on the sports page.

38. _____ Opinions do not belong in news articles.

39. _____ Antonyms are abbreviations.

40. _____ An interrogatory sentence ends with a question mark.

ABC **Take your LIFEPAC Spelling Test.**

Write four literary forms that come under the category of *nonfiction* (each answer, 3 points).

2.016 _____

2.017 _____

2.018 _____

2.019 _____

Match these synonyms (each answer, 2 points).

2.020 _____ panic

2.021 _____ genuine

2.022 _____ feed

2.023 _____ hedge

2.024 _____ specimen

2.025 _____ painful

2.026 _____ ignite

2.027 _____ stern

2.028 _____ breeze

2.029 _____ boring

a. clipped bushes

b. sample

c. set fire to

d. uninteresting

e. grim

f. fear

g. considerate

h. authentic

i. hurting

j. nourish

k. draft

Complete these sentences with the correct antonyms (each answer, 1 point).

| decline | ascend | barren | combine |
| accept | descend | fertile | separate |

2.030 I had to use a ladder to _____ from the roof.

2.031 I had to _____ the invitation because of illness.

2.032 The ground was quite _____ because of the low rainfall.

2.033 If you would _____ the two classes, everyone could see the film.

2.034 If dogs are fighting, do not try to _____ them.

2.035 Please _____ my apology as I really am sorry.

Answer true or false (each answer, 2 points).

2.036 _____ Frowns and smiles are forms of body language.

2.037 _____ If you are looking for a job, turn to the classified ads.

2.038 _____ A dust jacket is necessary to keep the dust off you.

2.039 _____ The main characteristic of journalistic writing is simplicity.

2.040 _____ Propaganda is a form of prop checking.

2.041 _____ A business letter has to be completely informal.

2.042 _____ Letters to the editor are one way of knowing how a community feels about issues.

Complete these statements (each answer, 3 points).

2.043 As a literary form Biblical _____ is unique.

2.044 The Ten Commandments are found in _____ .

2.045 The literary device used in Hebrew poetry is _____ .

2.046 The historical books of the New Testament are the four Gospels and _____ .

80 / 100 SCORE _____ TEACHER _____ _____
initials   date

ABC **Take your spelling test of Spelling Words-2.**

3. SECTION THREE

This section will review the simplest patterns of sentence structure. It will cover the essential parts of a sentence, such as the subject, the predicate, noun and verb phrases, adjectives and adverbs, and the expanded sentence.

You will also review capitalization, punctuation, prefixes, and suffixes. Different kinds of sentences, such as the declaratory, the interrogatory, the exclamatory, and the imperative sentence forms will be covered, as well as various spelling patterns.

Section Objectives

Review these objectives. When you have finished this section, you should be able to:

10. Identify sentence patterns and apply grammatical rules.

11. Identify and apply the rules of punctuation.

12. Identify and apply common spelling patterns.

Vocabulary

Study these words to enhance your learning success in this section.

colloquial (ku lō kwē ul). Informal speech acceptable and correct in ordinary conversation.

hieroglyphic (hī ur u glif ik). Ancient picture writing.

inflection (in flek shun). A change in pitch or tone of the voice.

ingredient (in grē dē unt). Any part of a mixture.

Pronunciation Key: hat, āge, cãre, fär; let, ēqual, tėrm; it, īce; hot, ōpen, ôrder; oil; out; cup, pùt, rüle; child; long; thin; /ŦH/ for then; /zh/ for measure; /u/ or /ə/ represents /a/ in about, /e/ in taken, /i/ in pencil, /o/ in lemon, and /u/ in circus.

PATTERNS IN LANGUAGE

We see our world in patterns. We demand order so that things will make sense to us. We classify our world. Animals, plants, cloud formations, in fact, all of nature, is seen in terms of patterns and classification. Rocks are just rocks to the average person, until he has a course in geology. Then rocks take on new characteristics, filling him with a sense of wonder. Similarly, words are just words until we realize that not only what we say but how we say it can affect those with whom we communicate. Patterns in language make learning easy.

Different languages have different sentence structures.

In German and Latin, the verbs are placed at the end of a sentence.

> Example: The fat cat on the mat sat.

In French, colors are placed after the noun, not before.

> Example: The cat brown sat on the mat blue.

In Hebrew the verb is placed first in the sentence.

> Example: Sat the cat on the mat.

Some languages are written in columns, others (like the Egyptian **hieroglyphics**) are in picture form. The English language has its own patterns, and we will review these patterns in this section.

Subjects and predicates. The simplest pattern to be seen in the English sentence is the subject (who or what we are talking about) and the predicate (what they are doing). Look at the index cards down below.

Find the verb, or action word, and that is where the separation of the subject and predicate occurs.

Even if you turn the sentence around, the break still occurs with the verb.

> Example: *The fat **cat** / sat on the mat.*
> *On the mat **sat** / the fat cat.*

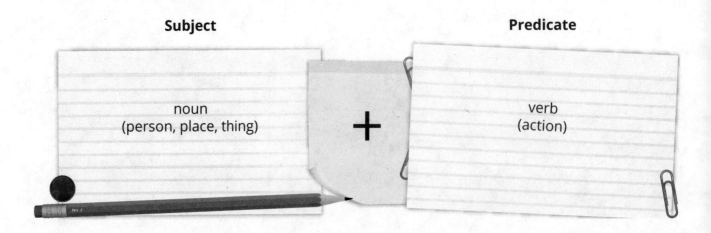

Subject

noun
(person, place, thing)

+

Predicate

verb
(action)

Circle the noun and the verb, and separate them with a line to show the subject and predicate. In two of the sentences, the subject and predicate are reversed.

3.1   A glorious light flashed through the darkness.

3.2   The ignorant man wanted to understand the book.

3.3   The sleepy bee buzzed around the petals of the flower.

3.4   Through the darkness flashed a glorious light.

3.5   Around the petals of the flower buzzed the sleepy bee.

Noun phrases and verb phrases. A phrase is a group of words that do not make complete sense by themselves, just as the subject does not make complete sense without the predicate, or vice versa. Now let us look at the index cards again. The group of words that explains or describes the noun is called a noun phrase. The group of words that explains, describes, or completes the verb is called a verb phrase.

Let us now look inside the phrases and break up the pattern and form new patterns.

Subject is a noun phrase

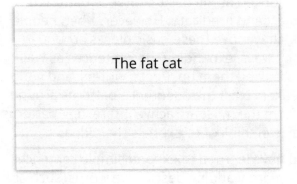

The fat cat

Predicate is a verb phrase

sat on the mat.

Adjectives. The words in front of the noun are called adjectives because they go with or describe the noun. One way to guess that a noun is very near, is to notice the three words *the*, *a*, and *an*. These words are special adjectives called definite and indefinite articles, but for the moment just call them adjectives. These three words signal a noun will follow.

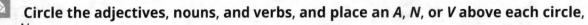

N

Circle the adjectives, nouns, and verbs, and place an *A*, *N*, or *V* above each circle, as in (cat). Separate the subject and predicate with a line.

3.6 The beautiful, rosy apples lay all over the floor.

3.7 The old book fell on the floor.

3.8 The prophet Daniel faced the lions in their den.

3.9 The old man painted the door a bright color.

3.10 Ten little monkeys played in the trees.

Adverbs. The predicate sometimes contains only the verb.

V

Example: She / (sang).

Often a word will be either before or after the verb which will tell you *how*, *when*, or *where* the action took place. These words are adverbs—they add something to the verb.

Examples of adverbs:

She / sang (quietly). (tells *how*)

She / sang (yesterday). (tells *when*)

She / sang (here). (tells *where*)

Sometimes an adverb will come between a helper verb and a verb.

H.V. Adv.   V

Example: "He (did)(not)(come)."

Interesting sentence patterns. So far you have only looked at the basic sentence pattern of subject and predicate. However, when people talk, they move these basic pieces around in many ways, expanding the sentences as well as breaking them up. Poets, writers, and good speakers twist their sentence patterns around to form the most attractive interesting patterns they can think of to express their ideas.

You have learned to expand simple sentences this year by adding descriptive words, such as adjectives and adverbs. You can expand the sentence by attaching more phrases. The subject and predicate are beginning to look even more complicated.

Subject

The cat, wide-eyed and watchful,

Predicate

sat patiently, tail twitching,
on the faded doormat.

When you start moving words out of their basic pattern or if you add phrases, you usually indicate the changes by using commas (as shown in the diagram). The predicate now has three verbs. To decide which verb is the main verb of the predicate, ask yourself (a) Who am I talking about? (the cat); then (b) What is the cat doing? (sitting). Consequently *sat* is the main verb and beginning of the predicate.

Circling words with different colored crayons helps you see how the words are used in the sentence. Use the following colors.

adjectives: red

adverbs: brown

nouns: blue

prepositions: yellow

verbs: green

The positioning of the colors should help you remember the usual order of words. You can see the pattern our words make when we speak. Your basic sentence pattern will give this color combination:

The   cat   sat   quietly   on   the   mat.
Adj.   *N.*   *V.*   *Adv.*   *Prep.*   *Adj.*   *N.*

Even when sentences are twisted around, the red (adjective) will nearly always come before the blue (noun). Brown (adverb) will usually come before or after the green (verb). Yellow (preposition) will always come before a red (adjective) + a blue (noun).

Helpful doodling. Whenever you have a few moments to spare, get out a magazine and circle the different parts of speech in advertisements. Play a game with a friend, seeing who can circle the most adjectives and nouns or some other part of speech. You will find it can be fun.

Old Hunting Recipe for Bison Stew

1	very old Bison
3	over-ripe onions
1	Australian hare
	A pinch of salt
	A lot of water

The first step is to shoot the bison. Next, find a cooking container large enough to hold it. Then let the carcass age in the sun for three weeks. If the body starts to attract flies, you know it is time to start cooking. Slowly bring the animal to a boil, parboil it for an hour, then reduce the heat. Let the stew simmer for a week until the meat is very tender.

Make sure there is enough water to cover the animal, as lengthy cooking tends to cause the water to evaporate. Finally, chop the three onions, then crush them before adding them to the stew. The onions give the stew more flavor. A pinch of salt is necessary to take away the wild taste of the animal. Add the hare (or rabbit, if the hares are not available) during the last forty-five minutes of cooking. For those who do not like hare in their stew, omit this **ingredient**.

Complete these activities.

3.11 Circle the words of the "Old Hunting Recipe" with colored crayons.

adjectives: (red)   adverbs: (brown)

nouns: (blue)   prepositions: (yellow)

verbs: (green)

3.12 List all the nouns, adjectives, verbs, and adverbs, pronouns and prepositions that are in the title, the ingredients, and the first paragraph of the "Old Hunting Recipe." Do not repeat words you have already noted, and omit the adjectives *the*, *an*, and *a* as they occur too frequently. Check the list of **prepositions** given in Language Arts LIFEPAC 608.

Nouns
_____   _____   _____   _____
_____   _____   _____   _____
_____   _____   _____   _____
_____   _____   _____   _____
_____   _____   _____   _____

Adjectives
_____   _____   _____   _____
_____   _____   _____   _____

Verbs
_____   _____   _____   _____
_____   _____   _____   _____
_____   _____   _____   _____
_____   _____   _____   _____

Adverbs
_____   _____   _____

Pronouns
_____   _____

Prepositions
_____   _____   _____
_____   _____

Answer this question.

What is the pun in the last four lines of the "Old Hunting Recipe?"

3.13 The play of words (or pun) is on the word _____

_____

PUNCTUATION

Punctuation is necessary in order to have written words make sense.

Punctuation symbols —

.   shows when a speaker or character takes a breath or is silent

,   starts a new thought

?   express doubt or uncertainty

!   says something sharply or talking about something special

" "   marks either the beginning and end of a title or quoted passage, word, or phrase being discussed

( )   inserted as an explanation or afterthought

:   introducing a quotation or list of items, separating two clauses of which the second expands or illustrates the first

;   indicates a pause, typically between two main clauses, more pronounced than that indicated by a comma

Look at the following sentences.

> "Snoopy! Where are you?
> Good grief, animal! Get out of that closet!"

If Charlie Brown, or anyone else, were saying this sentence, he would use a great deal of expression. Also probably there would have been a silence after the words "Where are you?" as he looked for the dog and opened the closet door.

Without punctuation all the words would have run together like this:

> snoopy where are you good grief animal get out of that closet

The sentence would have been hard to read. It would also be too awkward and tiring to read it if it were written like this:

> "Snoopy (character speaks sharply) where are you (his voice rises in a question) (silence as he looks in closet) good grief animal (very cross) get out of that closet (ordering Snoopy about)."

If books were written in such a fashion, they would take too long to read. We also do not enjoy having every action or voice **inflection** written out in detail for us. We like to do a little thinking of our own.

Purpose. Punctuation is a shorthand, or a short way, of writing a great deal of information. Listen to the way you speak. You take quick breaths (shown by commas) when you break up your sentence patterns; longer breaths and silences when you wait for a reply or think of something further to say (shown by periods, exclamation marks, and question marks). Punctuation is a convenient way of showing pauses, indicating loudness of voice or anger, and rising voice inflections when asking a question. Punctuation follows certain rules, and the rules are easy once you learn them.

Pointers. You have covered the rules of punctuation and capitalization throughout the year, and you will now review them.

a. Capitalize important or special names and titles, days of the week, names of the months, the word I, and the beginnings of a sentence.

b. *Interrogatory* sentences ask questions. They start with a verb or who, why, where, when, etc. and end with a question mark.

c. *Exclamatory* sentences show impatience or exclaim about something. They usually start with a **colloquial** expression, or a name of a person, and end with an exclamation mark.

> Example: "Snoopy! Good grief, animal!"

d. *Declarative* sentences are statements, and they end with a period. Most sentences are declarative sentences.

e. *Imperative* sentences state a request or command and end with a period.

> Example: "Get out of that closet."

f. Put your punctuation inside the quotation marks when indicating speech.

g. Put commas between numbers, especially when writing dates.

> Example: January 1, 1978

h. When writing a list, or series, place commas between each word of the list, and in front of the *and* before the last word of the series.

> Example: Inside the bag I found cats, dogs, rats, and mice.

Try to keep these punctuation pointers in mind as you complete the following activities and as you write material for your mini newspaper.

Complete this activity.

3.14 In each of the following sentences, certain words should be capitalized.
Circle the letters that need to have capitals.

a. On wednesday, uncle john is flying in from denver, colorado.

b. tomorrow is the first day of september and i have to leave for new york.

c. the amazon river is the largest river in the world and it is in brazil.

d. tom and jerry are cartoon characters like sylvester, the cat, and tweetie pie, the bird.

e. my brother and i went to cedar city high school this december.

Add the correct punctuation mark to the end of each sentence.

3.15 When I say jump, jump _____

3.16 I have to complete three essays _____

3.17 Wow _____ It tastes great _____

3.18 Have you seen my book anywhere _____

3.19 Johnny, do as I say _____

3.20 I saw many different kinds of birds today _____

3.21 Watch out _____ There's a snake _____

3.22 How are you going to get there in time _____

Rewrite the following three sentences on the lines and include all the missing punctuation and capitalization.

3.23 go away susan said her big sister I m very busy

_____

3.24 Jumping crickets it s hot why didn't you tell me said peter

_____

3.25 will you come back david said john

_____

SPELLING

Your spelling words were taken from Language Arts LIFEPACs 605 and 606. Notice that a variety of spelling patterns have been used. The hyphenated words and abbreviations come from Language Arts LIFEPAC 605. Plural words showing the rule of changing the *f* into a *v* and the words showing the different sounds of the letter *g* also come from Language Arts LIFEPAC 605. The homonyms were all taken from Language Arts LIFEPAC 606.

Review or learn the spelling of the words in Spelling Words-3.

━ SPELLING WORDS-3 ━

Review Words-605

by-products	reign	siege	father-in-law
capt.	tongue	dept.	indignant
hooves	so-called	knives	shelves
league	etc.	geese	illus.
ave.	thieves	submerge	vice president
surgeon	guest	blvd.	halves

Review Words-606

bail	reign	idol	soul
gait	waive	bale	wave
idle	cue	bored	gambol
sole	peace	gate	sore
board	soar	mourn	piece
morn	gamble	rain	queue

 Complete these three activities from Review Words-605 Spelling Words.

3.26 List the three hyphenated and one open compound spelling words.

a. _____   b. _____

c. _____   d. _____

3.27 List the five spelling words that have changed the *f* into a *v* in the plural form.

a. _____   b. _____

c. _____   d. _____

e. _____

3.28 Write the six spelling words that are abbreviations and their complete words. Use a dictionary if necessary.

a. _____   b. _____

c. _____   d. _____

e. _____   f. _____

Complete these activities from Review Words-605 Spelling Words.

3.29 List the four words that have a hard */g/* sound.

a. _____   b. _____

c. _____   d. _____

3.30 List the three words that have the soft */g/* sound.

a. _____ b. _____ c. _____

3.31 List the word that has a silent *g*. _____

3.32 List the *g* word that sounds like */ng/*. _____

Complete this activity.

3.33 List the twelve pairs of homonyms from Review Words-606 Spelling Words.

a. _____   b. _____

_____   _____

c. _____   d. _____

_____   _____

e. _____   f. _____

_____   _____

g. _____   h. _____

_____   _____

i. _____   j. _____

_____   _____

k. _____   l. _____

_____   _____

Prefixes. Prefixes are placed in front of a root word. One group of prefixes you have studied are negative prefixes, such as *un-*, *in-*, *im-*, *il-*, and *ir-*. They add the meaning *not* to the word.

Suffixes. Throughout the year you have studied the following suffixes: *-ish, -al, -less, -ment, -ive, -y, -able, -en, -ible, -ic, -ful, -ion, -s, -ance, -ence, -ant, -ent, -est, -er, -ing,* and *-ed*. Suffixes are endings attached to a root word.

Complete these activities.

3.34 Complete the following words by adding a negative prefix.

a. _____ polite   b. _____ reverent   c. _____ grateful

d. _____ possible   e. _____ sincere   f. _____ logical

g. _____ fair   h. _____ correct   i. _____ moderate

j. _____ resolute   k. _____ legible   l. _____ clean

3.35 Rewrite each word with several different suffixes. The number of different suffixes to be used for each word will be put in parentheses. Try to use other suffixes than *-s*.

a. dear (3) _____

b. hope (4) _____

c. please (4) _____

d. companion (2) _____

e. express (4) _____

f. light (5) _____

_____

ABC   **Ask your teacher to give you a practice spelling test of Spelling Words-3.** Restudy the words you missed.

Review the material in this section in preparation for the Self Test. This Self Test will check your mastery of this particular section. The items missed on this Self Test will indicate specific areas where restudy is needed for mastery.

SELF TEST 3

Write an *S* if the sentence fragment is a subject (noun phrase) or a *P* if it is a predicate (verb phrase) (each answer, 2 points).

3.01 _____ the weary little boy

3.02 _____ traveled for over an hour

3.03 _____ was feeling unwell

3.04 _____ a wide stretch of ice

3.05 _____ will be visiting us this fall

3.06 _____ Thanksgiving, a special holiday,

3.07 _____ faced the lions in their den

Add the correct punctuation mark at the end of each sentence (each answer, 2 points).

3.08 You must be joking _____

3.09 Where did you go on your holiday _____

3.010 Get on the horse and ride _____

3.011 Fifteen people came to the party _____

3.012 Did you ask your principal if you could go _____

3.013 Watch out _____

3.014 How long do you think you'll be _____

Write the complete words of these abbreviations (each answer, 3 points).

3.015 capt. _____

3.016 dept. _____

3.017 illus. _____

3.018 ave. _____

3.019 etc. _____

3.020 blvd. _____

Change these words into their plural forms (each answer, 2 points).

3.021   hoof   _____

3.022   half   _____

3.023   wife   _____

3.024   loaf   _____

3.025   wolf   _____

3.026   thief   _____

3.027   knife   _____

Write the nouns, adjectives, verbs, adverbs, and pronouns from these sentences on the lines (each word, 1 point).

Tired men and women walk slowly.
We came to the spooky house.

3.028   nouns (3)

a. _____   b. _____   c. _____

3.029   adjectives (3)

a. _____   b. _____   c. _____

3.030   verbs (2)

a. _____   b. _____

3.031   adverbs (1)

a. _____

3.032   pronouns (1)

a. _____

Write the source where you would go to find the following information (each answer, 2 points).

3.033 _____ an alphabetical list of words or subjects with the passages in which they are used

3.034 _____ verse by many authors

3.035 _____ the history of Quebec City

3.036 _____ the meaning of the word *adjectival*

3.037 _____ the dates of full moons in 1984

3.038 _____ a synonym for the word *despair*

3.039 _____ the achievements of Helen Keller

a. dictionary

b. thesaurus

c. almanac

d. concordance

e. an atlas

f. encyclopedia

g. *Who's Who*

h. anthology

Match the following items (each answer, 2 points).

3.040 _____ national or world news

3.041 _____ personal letters

3.042 _____ form of communication

3.043 _____ advertisements use it

3.044 _____ house and car sales

3.045 _____ balanced sentences

3.046 _____ business letter

3.047 _____ Ten Commandments

a. classified ads

b. basic code of Law

c. formal greetings

d. parallelism

e. obituaries

f. front page

g. informal greetings

h. propaganda

i. body language

80 / 100   **SCORE** _____ **TEACHER** _____ _____

initials   date

ABC   **Take your spelling test of Spelling Words-3.**

4. SECTION FOUR

This final section of the LIFEPAC will review the need for organization in all literary forms. You will review sequence of events, the main ideas of paragraphs, note-taking, and a short story.

You will also review further spelling patterns and spelling changes in suffixes of comparison and in verb tenses. The highlight of this section and of the Review LIFEPAC is the display of your mini newspaper.

Section Objectives

Review these objectives. When you have finished this section, you should be able to:

6. Take notes and organize them.
7. Describe and use the various elements of a story.
8. Write a short story and an essay.
9. Identify and use sources of information.
12. Identify and apply common spelling patterns.
13. Identify vowel digraphs, and homonyms, antonyms, and synonyms.

Vocabulary

Study these words to enhance your learning success in this section.

distracting (dis trak ting). Drawing attention away from something.

energetic (en ur jet ik). Having energy; active.

essential (u sen shul). Very important; cannot do without it.

disarray (dis u rā). A state of disorder.

react (rē akt). To act in response to a stimulus.

Pronunciation Key: hat, āge, cãre, fär; let, ēqual, tėrm; it, īce; hot, ōpen, ôrder; oil; out; cup, pu̇t, rüle; child; long; thin; /ŦH/ for then; /zh/ for measure; /u/ or /ə/ represents /a/ in about, /e/ in taken, /i/ in pencil, /o/ in lemon, and /u/ in circus.

ORGANIZATION IN LITERARY FORMS

All written communication, whether prose or poetry, needs a basic framework, in order for the reader or audience to have some sense of logical direction. The writer needs to organize his thoughts or ideas in such a way that there is a natural progress or easily understood flow from one idea to the next. It can be most **distracting** for the reader if thoughts are scattered about in **disarray**. The whole point of the passage may be lost.

When writing reports, essays, stories, newspaper articles, or fiction, organization is **essential**. Here are the six major steps a writer should take when creating a literary project.

1. Choose the topic.
2. Gather information.
3. Locate all sources of information.
4. Take notes.
5. Outline and organize the information.
6. Write the literary piece.

Note-taking. The writer does not have time to wade through pages and pages of notes to locate essential information. When information is gathered, much of it is not needed when the report is finally written. It is therefore necessary to be able to sort through and locate the main ideas hidden in your pile of notes. For this reason a skeleton framework is needed. The following points should be kept in mind when you are making notes.

1. Write your notes on cards.
2. Write down the questions that need to be answered in your report or essay.
3. Write down the main ideas or points you want to make.
4. Do not write complete sentences.
5. Use headings and subheadings to separate all the main ideas.
6. Number your points of information or examples to show the order they will follow.
7. Write down your references or sources of information.

Sources of information were studied in Section Two of this LIFEPAC. Knowing your sequence of ideas is half the battle in writing. Before you can give substance or structure to your work, however, you must have a desire or interest to share your ideas with others.

Complete this activity.

4.1 Turn back to Section Three of this LIFEPAC and reread the "Old Hunting Recipe for Bison Stew." Then complete the following basic framework for the recipe by making your own notes.

(Heading) Old Hunting Recipe for Bison Stew

(Subheading) Ingredients

_____

_____

_____

_____

_____

(Subheading) Cooking steps

_____

_____

_____

_____

_____

_____

_____

_____

_____

_____

_____

_____

TEACHER CHECK _____ _____
                              initials   date

Short story construction. Novels and short stories need as much organization and sequence of ideas as do reports and essays. They also need a sequence of events, which is called a plot. In Section Two of this LIFEPAC, the following elements of a short story were discussed: exposition, conflict, rising action, climax, falling action, and resolution.

The characters and the problems they are having are at the center of every story. The more fascinating the characters and the more difficult the problem, the more exciting the story. The plot centers around the characters and the problem. The way the characters **react** to and handle the problem is what controls the plot. For example, an **energetic** person would cope with a robbery in a different way than a lazy person.

Once you have outlined your story into the six elements, you need to outline your sequence of events (plot) that lead to the climax. When you have outlined the framework of your story, plunge right into the middle of the scene. Do not give huge passages or lumps of information because you could distract the reader and even bore them. It is better to scatter your information throughout the story.

Let us use "Little Red Riding Hood" as an example. The story starts off with Red Riding Hood's mother asking the little girl to take some goodies to her sick grandmother. We do not need to know whether Red Riding Hood has twenty-seven freckles on her nose or if she ate onions soaked in milk for breakfast. The writer does not have to tell us everything. The main thing is to get on with the story. Set the mood and the scene where the main action is to take place, such as the forest.

The description of the setting is made much more effective if we see how the character reacts to it. If we know how Red Riding Hood feels, and if we are told how she reacts, (she shivers; she hears the sound of cracking twigs; she feels goose bumps up her back), then the darkness of the woods is much more

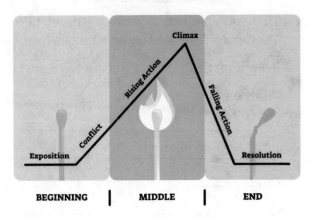

PLOT DIAGRAM

frightening. A good rule to remember, is to show, not tell, what is happening.

Editing process. Part of your organization process is to edit your work after the first draft. At first, write your ideas down as fast as you can. Do not stop to think about spelling or choice of words. Then (if you have time) put the story or report aside for a few days. When you look at it again, be critical. Take out all unnecessary words. Look in a thesaurus to find synonyms that you can use to replace some of your words. Good synonyms will add variety to your writing. Continual repetition of words in a passage is unimaginative and consequently, boring.

Look at your sentence patterns. Can you vary them?

Example: "Miriam, the cat, sloe-eyed and sleek, like some silken oriental pillow, sat on the mat by the door."

Notice that we still have the basic sentence of "the cat sat on the mat" but we now have some sort of mental picture of the animal. Do you notice the repetition of sounds and also the commas around the inserted phrases?

Try to use all these editing techniques and story techniques, as you finalize and polish up your mini newspaper, which must be completed by the end of the LIFEPAC.

Complete this activity.

4.2 Fill in your own descriptions of the plot, setting, problem, characters, climax, and outcome of the short story you will write for your mini newspaper. Put everything in note form.

Main plot events	Setting	Conflict
_____	_____	_____
_____	_____	_____
_____	_____	_____
_____	_____	_____
_____	_____	_____
_____	_____	_____

Characters	Climax	Resolution
_____	_____	_____
_____	_____	_____
_____	_____	_____
_____	_____	_____
_____	_____	_____
_____	_____	_____

TEACHER CHECK _____ _____
                    initials   date

Write a short story.

4.3 Write your short story from the notes you made. Use the rough draft, edit, final draft plan. Get it ready to be put into your mini newspaper.

TEACHER CHECK _____ _____
                    initials   date

Complete this crossword puzzle.

4.4 You may need to review some figures of speech from Language Arts LIFEPAC 606.

Across

6. an acronym for Zoning Improvement Plan

8. a referee

12. Beowulf was a I _____ figure.

13. famous, medieval English poet

15. a mixed-up egg

16. an acronym for Literature Department

18. tulip - tu (reverse the li) - p

19. a psychological term meaning "me"

21. a heroic tale

22. When you nod, you mean _____ .

23. this _____ that

24. a way of speaking

28. our solar system's star

29. a prefix meaning not

31. etile backwards

33. alone

34. a plan of eating

37. the first woman

38. Cowboys sometimes sing this way.

39. a story with animals acting like humans (a literary form)

40. to jump

43. the soft section of an animal's paw

44. the German secret police (an acronym)

45. a pronoun

46. Russian for *yes*

Down

1. a kind of dictionary

2. He fought an English legendary hero.

3. where you live

4. person who lives in Turkey

5. rodents

7. solidified water

9. belonging to me

10. Some people write with their _____ _____ (an acronym).

11. antonym of late

14. a board game with many upright pieces

16. a kind of record (an acronym)

17. a wall that holds back water

20. opposite of plain (a vocabulary word)

25. beginning letter of your name

26. a way of communicating with Deity

27. The Sphinx told one.

30. a part of your head

32. safe to eat

35. a palindrome for the sound of a little bird

36. a mathematical process

38. an affirmative

41. an acronym for Anno Domini

42. short term for father

SPELLING

Your spelling words were taken from Language Arts LIFEPACs 607, 608, and 609. You will review many spelling patterns, as well as spelling changes in the tenses of verbs and in the suffixes of comparison.

Review or learn the spelling of the words in Spelling Words-4.

━ SPELLING WORDS-4 ━

Review Words-607

screamed	twenty-two	dear	fear
already	consequently	learn	searched
break	leaped	forty-four	eightieth
bear	treasures	deceitfully	necessity
hear	great	reaching	fiftieth
early	wear	unpleasant	righteousness

Review Words-608

earliest	effective	happier	hypothesis
analyze	persuasion	stethoscope	atmosphere
opinion	publicity	digestion	observation
recycle	craziest	busier	simplest
tissue	science	gentlest	
influence	friendliest	infection	

Review Words-609

automatic	congratulate	museum	inheritance
necessity	almost	customary	dictionary
exaggeration	international	acrostic	biographical
descriptive	drama	historical	imagery
lament	personification	prophecy	prophetic

Complete this activity.

4.5 Copy Review Words-609 Spelling Words in your best handwriting and in alphabetical order.

a. _____   b. _____

c. _____   d. _____

e. _____   f. _____

g. _____   h. _____

i. _____   j. _____

k. _____   l. _____

m. _____   n. _____

o. _____   p. _____

q. _____   r. _____

s. _____   t. _____

Complete these activities using Review Words-607 Spelling Words.

4.6 List all sixteen words with the digraph *ea* in alphabetical order.

a. _____ b. _____ c. _____ d. _____

e. _____ f. _____ g. _____ h. _____

i. _____ j. _____ k. _____ l. _____

m. _____ n. _____ o. _____ p. _____

4.7 List three *ea* words that have the long /ē/ sound.

a. _____ b. _____ c. _____

4.8 List three *ea* words that have the short /ĕ/ sound.

a. _____ b. _____ c. _____

4.9 List two *ea* words that have the long /ā/ sound.

a. _____ b. _____

4.10 List two *ear* words that rhyme with *air*.

a. _____ b. _____

4.11 List three *ear* words that rhyme with *year*.

a. _____ b. _____ c. _____

4.12 List three *ear* words that have the sound as in *earn*.

a. _____ b. _____ c. _____

Complete these activities.

4.13 List the four number words taken from Review Words-607 Spelling Words.

a. _____   b. _____

c. _____   d. _____

4.14 List the three words taken from Review Words-608 that have four syllables (or rhythm beats).

a. _____   b. _____   c. _____

4.15 List the seven spelling words from both Review Words-607 and Review Words-608 that changed the *y* at the end of the root word into an *i* plus a suffix.

a. _____   b. _____

c. _____   d. _____

e. _____   f. _____

g. _____

Degrees of comparison. Root adjectives and adverbs show degrees of comparison (what is good, what is better, and what is best) by adding the suffixes *-er* and *-est*. The names of the three degrees of comparison are positive (the root word), comparative (*-er*), and the superlative (*-est*).

Most words follow the regular form of keeping the root word and adding the suffixes *-er* and *-est*. For example, *fond*, *fonder*, and *fondest*. Other words have irregular forms, such as *good*, *better*, and *best*. In these words the root word has changed.

Complete these activities.

4.16 List the two comparative forms (end in *-er*) found in Review Words-608 Spelling Words.

a. _____   b. _____

4.17 List five words from Review Words-608 Spelling Words that show superlative forms.

a. _____   b. _____

c. _____   d. _____

e. _____

4.18 List the word from Review Words-608 that is an exception to the *i before e except after c* rule.

_____

4.19 Complete the following "degree of comparison" chart.

	Positive	Comparative	Superlative
a.		kinder	
b.	quiet		
c.			greenest
d.	dainty		
e.		braver	
f.			palest
g.	new		
h.		poorer	

Verb changes. Verbs are words of action. They can show either present action, future action, or past action. In Language Arts LIFEPAC 608 you learned to conjugate verbs and separate the tenses. The present tense is the root or base word. For example, I *sing*, I *write*.

When changing the tense of the verb, helper verbs (or auxiliary verbs) are added before the verb.

Examples:

> Past tense: I have written, I was writing, or I wrote
>
> Present tense: I am writing or I write
>
> Future tense: I will be writing or I will write

Helpful Hints

In deciding what helper or auxiliary verbs to use, remember to:

- Use such helper verbs as *had*, *have*, *has*, *was, been*, and *were* to show the past tense,

- Use *is*, *am*, and *are* in the present tense,

- Use *will*, *shall*, *should*, and *would* with the future tense, and

- Usually the suffix *-ed* is added to show the past tense, as in *clean* → *cleaned* (in most cases).

 Complete this activity.

4.20 Circle the helper (auxiliary) verbs in the sentences.

a. I am not sure, but I think he has gone to see his parents.

b. It was difficult to see if the boys had reached their destination.

c. Peter said he would go and see if the parcel had been delivered.

d. I shall go if you will come with me.

e. I am writing to my aunt who is staying in Alaska for the summer.

4.21 Complete the chart, showing the present and past tenses of the verbs. Look in the dictionary if you are in doubt.

	Present	Past
a.	give	
b.		became
c.	sing	
d.		wrote
e.	worship	
f.		swam
g.	eat	
h.	supply	

Class activity. Set up a mini newspaper display in the class. By now you should have completed your mini newspaper. If you have worked hard and with imagination, you newspaper should be a project you will be pleased with. Arrange with your teacher to have a panel of judges to award certificates to the best effort in as many categories as possible: Best Art, Best News Story, Best Advertisement, Best Cartoon, Best Joke, Best Sports Account, Best Crossword Puzzle, and so forth. No student can win more than one certificate. When you run out of categories, think up some Honorable Mentions so that everyone who has participated receives credit for his work. Organize the display with your friends.

ABC **Ask your teacher to give you a practice spelling test of Spelling Words-4.** Restudy the words you missed.

Before taking the last Self Test, you may want to do one or more of these self checks.

1. _____ Read the objectives. See if you can do them.

2. _____ Restudy the material related to any objectives that you cannot do.

3. _____ Use the **SQ3R** study procedure to review the material.
   a. **S**can the sections.
   b. **Q**uestion yourself.
   c. **R**ead to answer your questions.
   d. **R**ecite the answers to yourself.
   e. **R**eview areas you did not understand.

4. _____ Review all vocabulary, activities, and Self Tests, writing a correct answer for every wrong answer.

SELF TEST 4

Match the meaning of these terms (each answer, 2 points).

4.01	_____ setting	a. performers of action
4.02	_____ plot	b. result
4.03	_____ problem	c. the high point of action
4.04	_____ characters	d. organization
4.05	_____ climax	e. series of events
4.06	_____ outcome	f. an obstacle
		g. scene of action

Answer true or false (each answer, 2 points).

4.07 _____ Organization is essential only for nonfiction.

4.08 _____ Knowing your sequence of ideas is important in making a report.

4.09 _____ The plot of a story centers around the characters and the problem.

4.010 _____ A writer should tell, not show, what is happening.

4.011 _____ Editing is only necessary when writing short stories.

4.012 _____ As a literary form, Biblical prophecy is unique.

4.013 _____ Poetry is only found in the Psalms.

4.014 _____ The whole of the Old Testament is history.

4.015 _____ The Ten Commandments are found in Exodus 20:1–17.

Write the comparative and superlative forms of these words (each answer, 1 point).

		Comparative	Superlative
4.016	friendly	_____	_____
4.017	crazy	_____	_____
4.018	simple	_____	_____
4.019	early	_____	_____
4.020	gently	_____	_____

Write the past tense of each of these verbs (each answer, 2 points).

4.021   eat   _____

4.022   reply   _____

4.023   sniff   _____

4.024   run   _____

4.025   practice   _____

Write *F* for fiction or *NF* for nonfiction before each title (each answer, 2 points).

4.026   _____   "Robinson Crusoe"

4.027   _____   "The Encyclopedia Britannica"

4.028   _____   The Acts of the Apostles

4.029   _____   a book of Aesop's Fables

4.030   _____   "The Frog Prince"

Match these words with their meanings (each answer, 2 points).

4.031   _____   adjective

4.032   _____   predicate

4.033   _____   subject

4.034   _____   myth

4.035   _____   parable

4.036   _____   grimace

4.037   _____   propaganda

4.038   _____   formal

4.039   _____   cliché

4.040   _____   synonym

a.   persuasive techniques

b.   word that means the same as another word

c.   a word that describes or limits a noun

d.   following certain established rules

e.   the part of the sentence that tells what the subject does or says

f.   complicated sentence pattern

g.   word or phrase used too frequently

h.   what or who the sentence is about

i.   a facial expression

j.   an imaginary story that tries to explain the beginning of something

k.   a short, teaching story

Place *P* for predicate or *S* for subject in front of each sentence segment (each answer, 2 points).

4.041 _____ jumped quickly over the fence

4.042 _____ is unable to arrive in time

4.043 _____ twelve country gentlemen

4.044 _____ the sad-faced clown

4.045 _____ will give everyone some money

Complete this list (each item, 2 points).

4.046 List five of the six things you must take notes on before you start to write a story.

a. _____   b. _____

c. _____   d. _____

e. _____

$\frac{80}{100}$ **SCORE** _____   **TEACHER** _____ _____
                                            initials   date

ABC **Take your spelling test of Spelling Words-4.**

Before taking the LIFEPAC Test, you may want to do one or more of these self checks.

1. _____ Read the objectives. See if you can do them.
2. _____ Restudy the material related to any objectives that you cannot do.
3. _____ Use the **SQ3R** study procedure to review the material.
4. _____ Review activities, Self Tests, and LIFEPAC vocabulary words.
5. _____ Restudy areas of weakness indicated by the last Self Test.
6. _____ Review all Spelling Words in this LIFEPAC.